EXECUTIVE SUMMARY

Following news reports that the Federal Bureau of Prisons (BOP) had confined an inmate for 13 months past his correct release date, the Department of Justice (Department) Office of the Inspector General (OIG) initiated an examination of the BOP's process for ensuring federal inmates are released on their correct release dates and the incidences of releases before or after the correct release date due to staff error between 2009 and 2014. We found that of the 461,966 inmate releases between 2009 and 2014, the BOP categorized 157 as untimely due to staff error. We also learned that the BOP classifies a far greater number — 4,183 — as untimely for other reasons.

According to the BOP, the vast majority of non-staff error "untimely" releases were due to situations that are beyond its control, such as amended sentences that result in shorter sentences than the time an inmate had already served. Also, data and information we reviewed indicates that other entities inside and outside the Department may sometimes contribute to untimely releases. Although BOP officials told us that it was highly unlikely that staff error on the part of a Department entity contributed to any of the 4,183 cases, they could not rule out the possibility and we found that the BOP does not always have complete information about the circumstances of untimely releases to which other entities contribute. We therefore concluded that the Department should work with all relevant entities, both within and outside the Department, to review the full range of possible reasons for untimely releases and how to address those that are in any way preventable.

With regard to the 157 untimely releases that BOP categorized as due to staff error, 152 were late releases and 5 were early releases. We found that three of the late releases and three of the early releases involved an error resulting in more than 1 year of over- or under-served time by the inmate. Table 1 displays the number of days of over- or under-served time for the 157 untimely releases.

Table 1

**Number of Untimely Releases from Prison Caused by Staff Errors,
By Days Over- or Under-served,
2009 – 2014**

	Days Over or Under Served	2009–2014	Percent of Total
LATE RELEASE	0 to 30 Days	91	60%
	31 Days to 1 Year	58	38%
	1+ Years	3	2%
EARLY RELEASE	0 to 30 Days	1	20%
	31 Days to 1 Year	1	20%
	1+ Years	3	60%

Source: OIG analysis of untimely releases identified by BOP as due to staff error, calendar years 2009 – 2014

While the 157 untimely releases due to staff error was rare compared to the 461,966 releases by BOP during the 6-year period of our review (an error rate of

0.03 percent), the consequences of an untimely release can be extraordinarily serious. Late releases from prison deprive inmates of their liberty, while early releases can put communities at risk if the inmates are dangerous. Early releases also can harm an inmate and the inmate's family, particularly if the inmate's efforts to gain employment and reestablish ties with the community are interrupted by a re-arrest for the purpose of completing the sentence.

Late releases also are costly: in addition to BOP costs associated with the unauthorized period of incarceration, there is the potential for significant compensatory judgments to those inmates who suffered an unconstitutional deprivation of their liberty. For the 152 late releases, we estimated the total cost to the BOP, exclusive of litigation and settlement costs, to be approximately $669,814. In addition, between 2009 and 2015, the Department settled four lawsuits by inmates alleging untimely release, one for $90,000; another for $120,000; another for $295,000; and the fourth for $175,000. This does not include additional costs the Department incurred as a result of these cases, such as salary costs expended to handle the lawsuits.

Additionally, untimely releases, whether early or late, contravene judicial sentencing orders, yet the BOP does not have in place a process to consider whether to notify the sentencing court of an untimely release. We found that, for late releases, the BOP notifies the relevant U.S. Probation office but does not separately notify the sentencing court or the U.S. Attorney's Office that handled the case. For early releases, we found that BOP policy requires Wardens to notify "the appropriate Judicial Official(s)" when an inmate who is deemed to be a threat to the community is released early and when any inmate is released more than 30 days early. Despite this policy, we found no such notifications occurred for the four untimely early releases of 30 days or more that we reviewed.

We found that 127 of the 157 untimely releases due to staff error were the result of errors made at BOP's Designation and Sentence Computation Center (DSCC). (The DSCC performs the vast majority of sentence computations the BOP uses to determine an inmate's release date.) The other 30 untimely releases were the result of staff errors at non-DSCC entities, such as BOP institutions, BOP Residential Reentry Management field offices, Residential Reentry Centers (previously known as Community Corrections Centers), and private contract prisons.

Prior to 2005, when the BOP consolidated sentence computation functions in the DSCC, individual BOP facilities across the country had performed sentence computation. The BOP transitioned sentence computations to the DSCC in order to consolidate BOP sentence computation functions, reduce costs, and ensure consistent application of laws and BOP policies. This change also helped reduce the number of untimely releases caused by staff error. Based on BOP data, we determined that during the 6-year period from 1999 and 2004 there were approximately 344 untimely releases due to staff error (around 0.1 percent of all releases) compared to 157 (around 0.03 percent of all releases) between 2009 and 2014.

We concluded that the most common sentence computation errors resulted from incorrect application of jail credit, incorrect determinations of primary jurisdiction between federal and state custody, and errors relating to concurrent versus consecutive sentences for defendants with multiple unexpired incarceration sentences. We also found that poor communication with outside entities — including local jails, courthouses, state departments of corrections, Native American reservations, the U.S. Marshals Service, and others — resulted in DSCC staff not obtaining complete and accurate sentencing information or interpreting sentencing information incorrectly, leading to untimely releases.

The BOP has several processes in place to prevent untimely release. One is to conduct a final release audit 12 months prior to an inmate's scheduled release date to discover and correct any errors and to have the ability to account for any reduced sentence time. However, we found that in some cases 12 months is not early enough to discover and correct the error and prevent the untimely release. Specifically, 14 of the 19 errors discovered by final release audits might not have resulted in untimely releases had the audits occurred 18 months before the inmate's scheduled release date. Had the final release audit occurred 24 months prior to the release date, an additional 4 of the 19 errors might have been discovered in time to prevent the untimely release. Therefore, we recommend that BOP explore and implement additional sentence calculation processing or auditing strategies, taking into account that conducting final release audits only 12 months before an inmate's projected release date has led to preventable untimely releases.

We also noted that the DSCC holds education events that bring together officials from the DSCC as well as outside the BOP (including U.S. District Court Judges, Federal Public Defenders, and U.S. Probation Office staff) to inform them about topics relating to DSCC operations, such as sentence computations. In our judgment, these events could help prevent untimely releases if the BOP included factors that can affect its ability to release inmates on time, including showing attendees how conflicting information can lead to incorrect sentence computations.

This report contains three case studies profiling inmate releases that were more than 1 year late. The report also makes seven recommendations for the BOP to help reduce untimely releases due to staff error.

TABLE OF CONTENTS

INTRODUCTION

Background

Following news reports in late 2014 about an inmate's lawsuit against the Federal Bureau of Prisons (BOP) for confining him 13 months beyond his correct release date, the Department of Justice (Department) Office of the Inspector General (OIG) initiated a review of the BOP's processes for ensuring inmates are released on their correct release date.[1] We found that of the 461,966 inmate releases between 2009 and 2014, the BOP categorized 157 as "untimely" due to staff error and a far greater number — 4,183 — as untimely for other reasons. As discussed in this report, according to the BOP, the vast majority of non-staff error untimely releases were due to situations beyond its control, such as amended sentences that result in shorter sentences than the time an inmate had already served.

Because the incident giving rise to this review resulted from BOP staff error, we focused on analyzing untimely releases that the BOP attributed to staff error. The BOP identified 157 such cases, including 148 cases attributable entirely to the BOP or others under its direct control, such as employees of private contract prisons. The remaining nine cases were due to a combination of factors including BOP staff error, and we discuss these later in the report.

The BOP's Processes for Computing and Verifying Inmate Sentences

Each year, the BOP conducts approximately 153,309 initial computations and 91,475 updates to existing computations to determine inmate release dates, and the Designation and Sentence Computation Center (DSCC), located in Grand Prairie, Texas, performs the vast majority of them. The DSCC, which consists of approximately 330 employees, was created in 2005 to consolidate all BOP sentence computation functions into one office to reduce costs and to ensure consistent application of laws and BOP policies. Prior to 2005, individual BOP facilities across the country had performed sentence computations. Between 2005 and 2010, the BOP phased out sentence computation functions at BOP-operated facilities and transferred these functions to the DSCC.[2]

---

[1] Paul McEnroe, "Lost in Federal Prison – and Held 13 Months Too Long," *Star Tribune,* October 11, 2014, http://www.startribune.com/lost-in-federal-prison-and-held-13-months-too-long/278868951/ (accessed March 9, 2016). KTTC staff, "Man Kept Imprisoned 13 Months Past His Release Seeks Lawsuit," *KTTC,* October 13, 2014, http://www.kttc.com/story/26776178/2014/10/13/man-kept-imprisoned-13-months-past-his-release-seeks-lawsuit (accessed March 9, 2016). Associated Press, "Man Held 13 Months Too Long Sues Prison System," *Washington Times,* October 11, 2014, http://www.washingtontimes.com/news/2014/oct/11/man-held-13-months-too-long-sues-prison-system/ (accessed March 9, 2016). The BOP settled the inmate's civil suit for $175,000.

[2] Due to existing contracts, several private contract institutions continued to perform sentence computation functions after 2010. Currently, there are four private contract institutions that continue to perform sentence computations: Big Spring Correctional Center, Big Spring, Texas (contract ends March 2017); Reeves County Detention Center I/II, Pecos, Texas (contract ends

Continued

The DSCC divides sentence computation responsibilities among teams that compute the sentences for federal inmates sentenced in 1 or more of the 94 federal judicial districts. Within each team, Classification and Computation Technicians and Specialists (CC staff) perform the day-to-day sentence computation functions of the DSCC, including calculating inmate release dates.[3] As shown in the Figure, these functions are divided into three main steps (two for sentences less than 13 months) and take place at different phases of an inmate's incarceration. In addition to these steps, sentence computation updates are performed when a change to an inmate's sentence occurs after the initial computation and certification audit.

Figure

Sentence Computation Steps

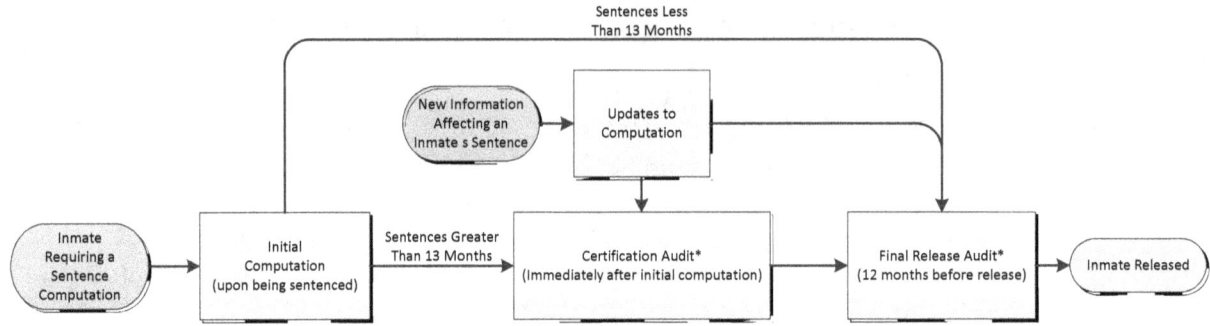

* The certification and final release audits follow the same procedure except that they ordinarily occur at two different stages of the inmate's incarceration.

Source: OIG analysis of sentence computations functions at the DSCC

Initial Sentence Computation

The CC staff calculates an inmate's release date at the beginning of the inmate's incarceration. During initial computations, the CC staff reviews a variety of source documents and SENTRY, the BOP's primary database for storing inmate information, to calculate the inmate's projected release date.[4] If any necessary

---

January 2017); Reeves County Detention Center III, Pecos, Texas (contract ends December 2016); and Taft Correctional Institution, Taft, California (contract ends August 2017). These institutions will transfer their sentence computation responsibilities to the DSCC when their current contracts end, the last of which will be in 2017.

[3] Classification and Computation Specialists and Technicians perform many of the same functions, but Specialists have more experience than Technicians, often answer the Technicians' questions regarding sentence computation, and can conduct the full range of sentence computation tasks. The DSCC provides CC staff basic and advanced training, on-the-job training, and quarterly training.

[4] Source documents include: a Judgment and Commitment Order describing the term of imprisonment and any other punishment the inmate faces; a Prisoner Custody, Detention, and Disposition Record (USM-129) from the U.S. Marshals Service (USMS), which notes where the USMS has moved the inmate after sentencing and before the BOP assigns the inmate to a facility and includes the inmate's time in custody during this period; and a pre-sentence report from the U.S. Probation Office in the sentencing jurisdiction, which usually includes the date the inmate was arrested and what dates the inmate was held in custody prior to sentencing. Other source documents that may

Continued

source documents are missing or incomplete, the responsible staff member will try to obtain them by contacting the appropriate state, local, federal, or other entity.

Certification Audit

The CC staff performs a certification audit after an initial computation and after computation updates to review the work of the staff member who conducted the computation, analyzing the same source documents. As an almost immediate check on the work of the staff member who conducted the initial computation or update, the staff member who performs a certification audit must be different from the staff member who performed the initial sentence computation. If information is missing, the staff member conducting the audit will typically direct the staff member who conducted the initial computation (or his or her replacement) to obtain the information.

Final Release Audit

Performed 12 months before an inmate's release date, the final release audit is designed to ensure that the sentence computation is correct, for example, that all updates have been incorporated, so that the inmate is released on his or her correct release date.[5] Because CC Specialists are more experienced than Technicians, only CC Specialists conduct final release audits. This audit is a final check on the initial computation and the certification audit, as well as any computation updates. The staff member conducting this audit will review the same source documents as those reviewed for the initial computation and certification audit. Similar to the certification audit, if necessary documentation is missing, the staff member conducting the final release audit will typically direct the staff member who conducted the initial computation to obtain the documentation.

Documentation of Untimely Releases

The BOP uses two forms to document untimely releases: the Untimely Release Notification (BP 558) and the Late Release Notice for United States Probation Service (BP 623). When an untimely release occurs, the BOP requires an employee from the office where the error occurred to complete a BP 558 form to document the untimely release, including an explanation of the reasons it happened and what has been done to make sure the mistake is not made again. If an inmate is subject to supervised release following a sentence from which the inmate was released late and accumulated over-served time, DSCC staff is also required to complete a BP 623 form and send it to the U.S. Probation Office. In this way, the

---

be used are the sentencing court's statement of reasons for the sentence and the inmate's National Crime Information Center report.

[5] Final release audits occur 12 months before an inmate's release to allow any decrease in the inmate's sentence that results from an error found by the audit to more likely be absorbed by the 12 months than to result in an untimely release.

BOP notifies the U.S. Probation Office that a court may consider the inmate's over-served time in calculating the prison time for a term of supervised release.[6]

Reviews of the DSCC

In addition to auditing individual sentence computations, the BOP's Program Review Division (PRD) conducts reviews of the DSCC and the DSCC conducts internal reviews of itself. The PRD conducts program reviews of all BOP programs in regular cycles where the cycle length depends on the rating the program received from the previous review. The PRD evaluates several areas of the DSCC, including sentence computations. The DSCC also conducts internal reviews, including reviews to assess actions taken to address areas of concern found during the PRD reviews.

Last, the DSCC conducts monthly audits, which it refers to as "perpetual" audits, for each sentence computation team. The perpetual audits review 170 (10 per team) randomly selected sentence computations that have undergone certification audits. The results of these perpetual audits provide information for quarterly reports and are the basis for in-house training. See Appendix 2 for additional details about the PRD and DSCC program review process.

Scope of the Review

In this review, we examined untimely releases of BOP inmates between calendar years 2009 and 2014 that the BOP classified as resulting from staff errors. Our report focuses on assessing the reasons for the untimely releases due to BOP staff error, the impact on the inmates, and their associated costs. We interviewed BOP officials, reviewed public and internal BOP documents, and analyzed data. During our assessment we also discovered releases that the BOP classified as untimely, due to a variety of reasons other than staff error, which can involve entities outside of the BOP. Although an in-depth analysis of the untimely releases not due to staff error was beyond the scope of this review, we describe the information we received regarding these as well. We offer recommendations at the conclusion of this report to assist the BOP and the Department in preventing and appropriately addressing untimely releases. Appendix 1 provides additional details about our methodology.

---

[6] Supervised release is a type of post-confinement monitoring overseen by federal district courts with the assistance of federal Probation Officers. A sentencing court is authorized (in some cases, required) to impose a supervised release in addition to imprisonment. While on supervised release after reentry into the community, an offender must abide by certain terms, some mandated by statute and others imposed at the court's discretion. Supervised release may be revoked if an offender violates a term. Upon finding such a violation, the court typically has discretion as to whether to require the offender to serve all or part of the supervised release term in prison. If an inmate who was released late and is subject to supervised release violates the terms of supervised release, the BOP will apply any time the inmate over-served toward the supervised release violation sentence. See 18 U.S.C. § 3585(b).

RESULTS OF THE REVIEW

The BOP Has Limited Information about the Causes of Releases Considered Untimely That Are Not Attributed to BOP Staff Error

We found that the BOP categorized 157 releases that occurred between 2009 and 2014 as untimely due to staff error, and a far greater number — 4,183 — as untimely for other reasons (a total of 4,340). BOP officials stated that most, if not all, of the untimely releases not attributed to staff error are beyond the BOP's control, either because an entity other than the BOP was responsible for or contributed to making the release untimely or because the untimely release was likely not preventable. For example, a BOP official told us that in many of these cases an inmate was released following a retroactive action that reduced his or her sentence to less time than he or she already had served. Under the BOP's current definition, any time served beyond the revised sentence is counted as "over-served time" and any release for which there is over-served time is counted as "untimely." We also observed that non-BOP entities can contribute to an untimely release even in instances where there is also BOP staff error. It was beyond the scope of this review to fully examine or assess untimely releases not attributed to staff error; however, we are concerned that because the BOP does not always have complete information about the circumstances of untimely releases that other entities contribute to, steps that could be taken to prevent them won't be identified.

We discussed with BOP officials the circumstances that might result in untimely releases that are not due to staff error and some of the actions the BOP takes to address these untimely releases. We found that while the Designation and Sentence Computation Center (DSCC) reviews every untimely release to determine whether there was staff error and classifies it into a general category by cause, the DSCC focuses on identifying actions that could prevent future BOP staff errors, rather than on understanding all possible contributing factors, including those outside of the BOP's direct control.[7] For this reason, the BOP does not systematically obtain the information it would need to determine with certainty the role other entities may have played. BOP managers told us that collecting this information would be laborious and that it may not be helpful in preventing untimely releases because, they believe, the vast majority of untimely releases are due to some form of technicality, such as the example of a retroactively reduced sentence provided above. Additionally, BOP managers stated that without thoroughly re-reviewing the 4,183 untimely releases not due to staff error, they could not be certain that any given untimely release could not have been prevented by one of the agencies involved.

Table 2 summarizes the BOP's classification and explanation of the untimely releases that occurred between fiscal year (FY) 2009 and 2014 and that it considers not due to staff error.

---

[7] One BOP manager indicated that any trend, regardless of whether it was due to staff error, would also be identified during the DSCC's review process.

Table 2

**Number of Untimely Releases by Cause, Not Including Staff Error
FYs 2009 – 2014**

BOP Classification	Definition/Explanation	Number of Untimely Releases
Federal Court Order/Amended Judgment	An order that was revisited and modified for either a legal or a judicial reason. Occasionally, these orders will be modified to include reducing the sentence. If the offender has already served more time than the new sentence imposes, the inmate becomes an immediate release and may have over-served time.	1,874
Federal Ineffectual Sentence	An ineffectual sentence occurs when the statutory release date is earlier than the date the sentence was imposed. This happens when a court sentences an offender based on Sentencing Guidelines and imposes terms that do not account for the period of time that the offender was held in official detention, instead of imposing a "time served" order.	596
U.S. Parole Commission Decisions	A U.S. Parole Commission decision may cause an untimely release when the statutory release date is earlier than the date of the Commission's decision.	165
"E-Des" Cases Submitted Late by the U.S. Marshals Service or U.S. Probation Office	This is a relatively new category of untimely release that the BOP began tracking in the fourth quarter of 2014. It occurs when the statutory release date is later than the date the sentence was imposed but earlier than the date the BOP received all the documents necessary to designate the inmate.	49
Untimely Releases with No Department Involvement	Any outside local or state agency that provides pre-sentence jail time and new or updated sentencing information after the inmate is in BOP custody may contribute to the inmate receiving credit the BOP did not previously provide. On occasion, a state entity might have its sentence overturned and vacated after the federal sentence has been computed, and the BOP then has to adjust the inmate's creditable time.	1,499
TOTAL		**4,183**

* The statutory release date is the date that a person must be released at the expiration of his or her term of sentence, less any time deducted for good conduct.

** Designation is the process of determining which BOP institution is to house an inmate. The BOP is solely responsible for determining where a federal offender will serve his or her sentence. To make a designation, the DSCC must first receive all sentencing material regarding the offender, including documents from the sentencing court, the U.S. Probation Office, and the U.S. Marshals Service (USMS). "E-Designate" is a system whereby the materials needed to designate inmates are shared between agencies electronically.

*** This table reflects the BOP's classification of untimely releases not due to staff error. We did not review the documentation associated with them or attempt to confirm the BOP's classification. The USMS noted that without reviewing the particulars of each of the 49 E-des cases, it could not verify that they were due to late submission.

Source: Untimely releases the BOP identified as not caused by staff error, FYs 2009 – 2014

The BOP explained that at the department level, the U.S. Marshals Service (USMS) and the U.S. Parole Commission, respectively, can contribute to causing untimely releases through either having custody of or granting parole for BOP inmates. Non-Department entities such as local and state agencies that had custody of an inmate prior to the BOP's custody can cause or contribute to untimely releases because the length of an inmate's sentence may be affected by overturned or vacated state sentences. To correctly update an inmate's release date, the BOP must receive timely and accurate sentencing information.

As shown in Table 2, the BOP attributed as many as 3,969 of the untimely releases during our review period to court orders and sentencing technicalities at the federal, state, or local level.[8] In addition to the situation described above about a release that was technically untimely even though no staff error contributed, DSCC officials presented examples to us of ways that sentencing orders can be written that leave room for the kind of confusion in computing sentences that can result in an untimely release. For example, on occasion sentencing orders are written in a manner that could appear to contravene governing law, such as sentences that appear to credit time spent in service of another sentence when the statute governing sentence calculation does not allow it.[9] This can create confusion about the point at which the beginning of the sentence should be calculated, thereby potentially leading to an untimely release.

One DSCC official told us that, when a sentencing judge's order is ambiguous, BOP Classification and Computation staff (CC staff) will try to reach the court for clarification. However, if the CC staff is unsuccessful in obtaining the information necessary to fully understand the order so that it can complete the computation within the DSCC's established time frame, the staff must interpret the order according to what it thinks the judge's intention is and move on to other cases. Another example a DSCC official described is that sometimes a judge may include instruction in a sentencing order about how to account for jail credit in a specific sentence. When this occurs, it can create a difference between what the inmate's sentence would be if the calculation was based on the judge's order and what the sentence would be if the BOP followed BOP policies, which, according to the BOP, are based on federal statute and case law.[10] We note, however, that addressing such issues only on a case-by-case basis rather than through system-wide changes precludes the implementation of changes that could prevent this type of error.

In the OIG's judgment, the fact that the BOP classified 4,340 releases (nearly 1 percent of all releases) as untimely during the period of our review, but only

---

[8] The 3,969 includes Federal Court Order/Amended Judgment, Federal Ineffectual Sentence, and Untimely Releases with No Department Involvement.

[9] See 18 U.S.C. § 3585(b).

[10] According to the BOP's Legal Resource Guide to the Federal Bureau of Prisons (2014), 12, the BOP is solely responsible for calculating federal terms of imprisonment. This guide lists the BOP's policies for calculating the terms of imprisonment as Program Statements 5880.28, Sentence Computation Manual (CCCA of 1984); 5880.30, Sentence Computation Manual ("Old Law" Pre-CCCA-1984); 5880.33, District of Columbia Sentence Computation Manual; and 5110.16, Administration of Sentence for Military Inmates. The guide notes that "occasionally, a 'Judgment and Commitment' may direct the defendant's term of imprisonment to be calculated in a manner contrary to law." In 1992, the U.S. Supreme Court held that a district court cannot award jail credit at sentencing (see *United States* v. *Wilson,* 503 U.S. 329 (1992)).

comprehensively assessed the 157 that it attributed to BOP staff error, demonstrates a need for further review of all untimely releases. We believe the BOP should be a central participant in such a review, but we also believe the review must include the many entities within and outside the Department that have roles in writing, interpreting, and executing judicial orders and other sentencing documents. Coordinated action is needed to identify and implement changes that would broadly address the significant problem of untimely release.

For such a review to provide a better understanding of the causes of untimely releases, information about the circumstances surrounding each untimely release, including, where applicable, the role that non-BOP entities played, must be available. However, in reviewing untimely release documentation, we found that the details of the circumstances that led to untimely release are not always complete enough to determine the cause of each case. This is especially true when a non-BOP entity may have contributed to the untimely release. The specific details needed to fully assess the untimely release are known only to the non-BOP entity that was directly involved, and the BOP does not uniformly have or include this information in its untimely release documentation. Improving the documentation of untimely releases, potentially by having all the agencies that contributed to a given untimely release provide explanatory information, may be a necessary first step toward a review.

Untimely Releases Due to Staff Error, While Rare in the Context of All Inmate Releases, Occurred Over 150 Times in a Recent 6-Year Period, Resulting in Significant Harm

Based on BOP data, we determined that between 2009 and 2014 there were 157 total untimely releases due to staff error out of the 461,966 total inmates released, representing 0.03 percent of all releases during that 6-year period.[11] We found that of the 157 untimely releases, 152 were late releases and 5 were early releases. Of the five early releases, three occurred in 2009 and were early by 955 days, 730 days, and 368 days, respectively; one took place in 2014 and was 31 days early; and one took place in 2013 and was 7 days early.

As shown in Table 3, of the 152 late releases during this period, 60 percent resulted in over-served time of less than 30 days and 40 percent resulted in over-served time of more than 30 days. Three of the inmates over-served by more than 1 additional year: these inmates over-served 928, 541, and 406 days,

---

[11] We found that 148 of these 157 untimely releases were due entirely to BOP staff error. The remaining 9 fell into the following categories: 2 resulted from a combination of BOP staff error and over-served time due to a sentence reduction or an ineffectual sentence (we excluded over-served days due to sentence reductions and ineffectual sentences from our analysis); 4 resulted from a combination of BOP staff error and USMS actions that we could not determine as staff error; 2 resulted from a combination of BOP staff error and either U.S. Probation Office or sentencing court actions that we could not verify were staff error; and 1 case in which we could not determine whether the BOP, the USMS, or both were responsible for the untimely release. The information we received from each agency about these untimely releases was not always detailed or conclusive enough to allow us to definitively determine the role of each agency or whether staff error was a contributing factor.

respectively. In addition, Table 3 shows that the percentage of releases that were late was relatively constant between calendar years (CY) 2009 and 2014.

Table 3

Late Releases Caused by Staff Error, by Year and Number of Days Late CYs 2009 – 2014

DAYS LATE	2009	2010	2011	2012	2013	2014	TOTAL
0-30	16	19	13	16	15	12	91
31-90	8	6	4	5	8	6	37
91-365	5	2	5	3	2	4	21
365+	0	1	0	0	2	0	3
Total Untimely Releases	**29**	**28**	**22**	**24**	**27**	**22**	**152**
Percentage of All Releases	0.04%	0.04%	0.03%	0.03%	0.03%	0.03%	0.03%

Source: OIG analysis of untimely releases identified by the BOP as caused by staff error, CYs 2009 – 2014

Untimely Late Releases Result in the Deprivation of Freedom and Contravene the Sentencing Court's Order

Untimely late releases are unjust. The length of a prison term is intended to be commensurate with the crime and other relevant facts of the case, as determined by the sentencing judge. When inmates are released later than their correct release date they are deprived of their freedom without just cause during the days they are over-serving. In the case that was the impetus for this review, a former BOP inmate filed suit and alleged he was falsely imprisoned because he was incarcerated beyond his release date.[12] The BOP settled with the inmate, and his case was dismissed. When untimely late releases occur, the harm to the inmate can be significant and irreparable.

Additionally, untimely releases, whether early or late, result in incarceration for less or more time than contemplated by the sentencing court. However, we found that while the BOP program statement contains a notification policy, it is not comprehensive and the BOP does not have in place a process to consider whether the sentencing court, as opposed to other offices within the court system, should be notified of an untimely release.

The BOP program statement setting forth the notification policy and requirements states:

> In any case involving an inmate's untimely release (including court ordered releases that are not acted upon in a timely manner) of 30 days or more and/or has been identified as a threat to the community [sic], the Warden must forward a personal letter to the

---

[12] *Hickman v. United States,* 14-cv-03041 (D. Minn.), filed July 30, 2014.

appropriate Judicial Official(s) providing details of the untimely release.[13]

To satisfy this policy for late releases, a BOP official told us that it completes and forwards a "BP-623: Late Release Notice for United States Probation Service" form to the appropriate U.S. Probation Office. The BOP sends these notices for all late releases, including those of less than 30 days. The BOP does not separately notify the sentencing court, and it does not notify the U.S. Attorney's Office that handled the case. One BOP official told us that the BOP does not notify the sentencing judge for untimely late releases because the term of imprisonment has been satisfied. With regard to notification to the inmates themselves, BOP Program Statement 5800.15 requires that a roster of sentence computation changes be given to unit teams each day, and that a copy of the inmate's sentence computation be sent to the inmate's file and the inmate. The Program Statement does not indicate if inmates are to be made aware that they have been held beyond their correct release date for any reason, and it was beyond the scope of this review to determine if that is done as a matter of practice.

For early releases, BOP officials told us that the BOP notifies the sentencing court specifically in cases in which an inmate has been released more than 30 days early, because of the threat the incorrectly released inmate may pose to the public safety of the community. However, we found that no such notifications occurred for the four early releases of 30 days or more that we reviewed. For three of these four cases, a BOP official told us that they did not notify the sentencing court because the inmates were returned to custody prior to the notification letter being drafted.[14] In the fourth case, a BOP official cited as the basis for not notifying the sentencing court the fact that the error resulting in the inmate's early release was not identified until after the inmate's correct release date had passed.

Given the sentencing court's inherent interest in ensuring that its orders are obeyed, in our judgment the Department should ensure that its components consider whether, in cases of early or late release due to staff error or any other reason, notification to the sentencing court would be appropriate. Such an effort would require that the BOP consult closely with other Department components, particularly the Executive Office for United States Attorneys, about the circumstances under which it might be appropriate to notify the courts and/or the specific U.S. Attorney's Office that handled a case that led to an untimely release.

---

[13] BOP Program Statement 5800.15, Correctional Systems Manual, January 1, 2009, Chapter 9, section 906.

[14] As discussed later in the report, of the five inmates mistakenly released early, one was out of custody for 14 days prior to being returned to custody, one for 5 days, and one for less than a full day. For the other two inmates, the correct release date passed while they were out of custody — one after 6 days and the other after 30 days.

Untimely Releases Result in Abrupt Reentry of Inmates into Society

When the BOP discovers that an inmate is erroneously over-serving time on an existing sentence, the inmate is immediately released to minimize the number of days over-served. Unfortunately, this may result in the release of inmates who are less prepared to reenter society than would have been the case if no error had been made. The BOP has a variety of programs geared toward preparing inmates for successful reentry; some are planned around an inmate's release date. For example, according to the BOP's Program Statement, participation in the Release Preparation Program begins 30 months prior to release and covers programming in six core areas: (1) Health and Nutrition, (2) Employment, (3) Personal Finance and Consumer Skills, (4) Information and Community Resources, (5) Release Requirements and Procedures, and (6) Personal Growth and Development.[15] With some exceptions, all inmates in the BOP's custody are required to participate in the Release Preparation Program.[16]

In addition to an untimely released inmate's inability to participate in the Release Preparation Program, an official from the Administrative Office of the U.S. Courts told us that an abrupt release makes the inmate's reentry, as well as the jobs of those who assist with the inmate's post-release supervision process, much more difficult. One DSCC official we spoke with suggested that abrupt reentries into society would be especially difficult for inmates who had been in prison for a long time.

Untimely Late Releases Result in Significant Monetary Costs to the Taxpayer

There are a number of significant monetary costs that result from untimely releases due to staff error, including the daily cost of incarcerating inmates beyond their correct release dates as well as any litigation and settlement costs.[17] We found that between 2009 and 2014, inmates over-served a total of 8,917 days due to staff error, at an estimated total cost of nearly $669,814 (see Table 4), exclusive of litigation and settlement costs. In aggregate, inmates over-serving time due to staff error in medium security facilities cost the BOP the most, at approximately $254,313; inmates over-serving time in administrative facilities cost the BOP the least, at approximately $6,364.[18]

---

[15] BOP Program Statement P5325.07, Release Preparation Program, December 31, 2007, paragraph 10.b. The BOP's Release Preparation Program is the subject of an ongoing OIG review.

[16] Inmates not required to participate include those committed for psychological study and observation (to assess their need for psychological treatment or services), those serving a sentence of 6 months or less, those with a death sentence, those confined in an administrative maximum security institution, those with a "Will Deport Order," state inmates, deportable aliens, and inmates arriving at their initially designated institution with less than 6 months remaining on their sentence.

[17] It was beyond the scope of our review to analyze the monetary costs resulting from untimely releases not due to staff error.

[18] The BOP's daily cost to house inmates depends on the security level: the higher the security level of the inmate, the greater the cost. Administrative facilities are institutions with special missions that house inmates at all security levels. Inmates are assigned to administrative facilities for

Continued

Table 4

**Estimated Incarceration Costs of Late Releases Due to
Staff Error, by Security Level
CYs 2009 – 2014**

	Number of Inmates	Total Days Over-Served	Total Cost to BOP
Minimum	18	484	$ 28,365
Low	64	3,474	$ 249,648
Medium	45	3,487	$ 254,313
High	21	1,390	$ 130,810
Administrative	2	77	$ 6,364
Unknown	2	5	$ 314
Total	**152**		**$ 669,814**

Source: OIG analysis of untimely releases identified by BOP as caused by staff error, CYs 2009 – 2014

In addition to the cost of incarceration, under the *Federal Tort Claims Act of 1946,* inmates may also seek monetary damages from the federal government for time over-served.[19] An inmate's first step in seeking compensation for being held beyond the correct release date is to file an administrative claim with the BOP. If the BOP denies the claim, or the inmate is dissatisfied with the BOP's settlement offer, the inmate may file suit in federal court.

Between 2009 and 2015, the federal government settled four lawsuits filed by inmates alleging untimely release.[20] These settlements were for $90,000; $120,000; $295,000; and $175,000.[21] According to the BOP, these were the only administrative or litigation settlements for untimely releases that the federal government paid during this period. This does not include additional costs the Department incurred as a result of these cases, such as salary costs expended to handle the lawsuits.

---

reasons other than security level, such as to be near a court where they are required to be present. To calculate the cost of an untimely release, we used the average daily cost to house an inmate at the inmate's security level during the year the inmate was released. There were two inmates who over-served a total of 5 days for whom the BOP could not identify the security level. We based the average daily cost on the fiscal year average of the total daily cost per inmate per day by security level, as provided by the BOP. We determined the number of days by the total number of over-served days for all late releases, by security level.

[19] Title VI of the *Legislative Reorganization Act of 1946,* codified at 28 U.S.C. § 1346(b) and 28 U.S.C. § 2671-2680.

[20] One additional lawsuit, filed between 2009 and 2014, was dismissed. In general, the relevant U.S. Attorney's Office handles litigation for untimely release lawsuits.

[21] These settlements were paid out of the U.S. Treasury Department's Judgment Fund.

Early Releases Result in Costs to the Department and the Taxpayer, as well as Potential Harm to Inmates, Their Families, and Their Communities

After an untimely early release occurs, the USMS locates and apprehends the inmate and then transports the inmate to a BOP facility to undergo intake processing. These actions cost the BOP and the USMS time and resources.

The potential harm can also be significant for the inmate, his or her family, and the community. For example, they may suffer harm if the inmate is rearrested after he or she has gained employment and reestablished ties with family and community. Also, the community into which the inmate is released early may be placed in danger if the inmate pursues criminal activity upon release. Though these potential harms exist, we determined that for the five early releases between 2009 and 2014, none of the inmates was rearrested, charged with, or convicted of any crimes during the time he or she was in the community before the correct release date. Additionally, none of the inmates mistakenly released was free for more than 30 days: three were out of custody for no more than 14 days; for the other two, the correct release date passed while they were out of custody — one after 6 days and the other after 30 days.

The Causes of Untimely Releases Vary

We found that most untimely releases due to staff error between 2009 and 2014 were the result of mistakes at the DSCC. However, other BOP entities and possibly the USMS also made mistakes that led to untimely releases. Of the 157 untimely releases between 2009 and 2014 that were within the scope of our review, the BOP classified 127 as the result of errors made at the DSCC and 30 as the result of errors at non-DSCC entities.

Untimely Releases as a Result of DSCC Staff Error

Even among untimely releases due to staff error, it was not possible to classify each untimely release by a single, mutually exclusive cause because some untimely releases were due to a combination of factors. Rather than comparing types of errors, we sought to highlight the mistakes that, if addressed, could make the most difference for reducing the number and severity of untimely releases. Below we explain the most significant types of errors and how they occurred.

In our review of each of the 127 untimely releases that the BOP classified as being due to DSCC staff error, we identified certain mistakes as most significant either because they occurred the most frequently or because they tended to result in a significant number of days over served. Specifically, misapplication of jail credit resulted in 59 of the 127 untimely releases — the most of any type of error we identified in our analysis. Our analysis also found that errors in identifying primary jurisdiction and consecutive versus concurrent sentences tended to result in a significant number of days over served. Specifically, the average number of days over served in untimely releases due to errors in identifying primary jurisdiction was 169 and those due to errors in determining consecutive versus concurrent sentences was 102 — the highest of any error type that we identified in our analysis. Below, we elaborate on the errors we believe are most significant based on our analysis of the 127 errors that occurred at the DSCC.

- **Misapplication of Jail Credit.** Correctly computing an inmate's release date depends on accurately determining the amount of jail credit the inmate has that should be applied to the sentence. Jail credit, also referred to as prior-custody credit, is typically the amount of time the inmate spent in local,

  > **Example of Misapplication of Jail Credit Resulting in Untimely Release**
  >
  > One untimely release was the result of the CC staff not following up on documentation that should have led the staff member to contact a local jail. A CC staff member reviewed a document that indicated the inmate may have been arrested for a probation violation, but the arrest was not verified in the document. This should have led the staff member to contact the jail where the inmate would have been held to ask whether the arrest had actually taken place and, if so, how many days the inmate had spent in jail. If the staff member had contacted the jail, he would have discovered approximately 1 month of additional jail credit. After the inmate made an informal request to review his release date, the DSCC discovered and applied the additional jail credit. Ultimately, the error resulted in a late release of 13 days.

  state, or federal custody after the date of offense and before commencement of the federal sentence. Once applied, this credit reduces the amount of time inmates must serve in the BOP. When it is not applied — or is applied incorrectly — it can result in an incorrect release date computation. We found that incorrect jail credit calculation by DSCC staff caused, in whole or in part, 59 of the 157 untimely releases within our scope between 2009 and 2014, making it by far the most frequent staff error-related cause of untimely releases during this period.

  Most of the DSCC staff we interviewed said that determining jail credit is the most difficult part of sentence computation because accurate calculation requires obtaining and analyzing information from other entities that held the inmate prior to BOP custody. Local jails, courthouses, state departments of corrections, and Native American reservations are some of the entities that DSCC staff may need to contact to obtain this information.

  We found three common causes of jail credit error attributable to BOP staff: (1) not following up to obtain or verify jail credit information; (2) failing to account for relevant information in the documents; and (3) not following up on relevant documentation in a timely fashion, the consequences of which are most pronounced for inmates with shorter sentences. See the text box above for an example of an untimely release caused by misapplication of jail credit.

- **Incorrect Interpretation of Source Documents.** As stated above, the CC staff analyzes documents to determine an inmate's date of release. Misinterpretation of one or more of these documents can lead to an incorrect release date computation. We identified two categories of errors stemming from a misinterpretation of source documents that were more frequent than others, which resulted in, on average, longer over-served time than other errors: (1) misidentification of primary jurisdiction and (2) misidentification of concurrent versus consecutive sentences.

- o *Primary Jurisdiction.* Several complications can arise when computing the sentence of an inmate subject to the authority of multiple jurisdictions. While complicated, especially when an inmate has multiple state and federal sentences and has been arrested and released by multiple state and federal authorities, correctly determining which jurisdiction has "primary jurisdiction" is essential for accurately computing an inmate's sentence. Generally the authority, whether federal or state, that first arrested the inmate has primary jurisdiction over the case. For example, if an inmate with federal and state charges pending is arrested by federal agents, the inmate is under primary federal jurisdiction. However, if the inmate posts federal bond and is released to state authorities, the primary jurisdiction can change to state jurisdiction. Primary jurisdiction can also be transferred if an inmate had been released on bail or parole, state charges are dismissed, or state and federal authorities make an agreement regarding custody.[22]

  Incorrect determinations of primary jurisdiction often result in inaccurate application of jail credit or an incorrect sentence start date, which can lead to an untimely release. We found that 9 of the 157 untimely releases within the scope of our review were the result, in whole or in part, from an incorrect determination of primary jurisdiction. These untimely releases resulted in an average of 169 days of over-served time, which is much higher than the average of 59 days of over-served time for all other untimely releases between 2009 and 2014. We describe a primary jurisdiction error below in Case 2 under Case Studies of Releases over 1 Year Late.

- o *Concurrent versus Consecutive Sentences.* If an inmate has been convicted of more than one crime, the two or more sentences can run concurrently (at the same time) or consecutively (one sentence begins after the other ends). We found that nine of the untimely releases within the scope of our review were, in whole or in part, the result of an incorrect determination of concurrent versus consecutive sentences. These errors resulted in an average of 102 days of over-served time, as compared to the average of 63 days of over-served time for all other untimely releases between 2009 and 2014. We also found instances where the DSCC staff mistakenly used the incorrect sentence type even when the correct sentence type was indicated in the documentation.

---

[22] In the BOP's comments to this report, the BOP stated that "DSCC staff determinations of sentence computations may be further complicated when federal sentencing courts expect the federal government to take a defendant into custody immediately upon sentencing, which is contrary to the training DSCC staff receive and the computation system utilized at the DSCC."

DSCC Communication with External Entities to Obtain Jail Credit Information

All of the CC staff members we interviewed, as well as many of the other DSCC staff members with whom we spoke, told us that communication with entities outside the DSCC to obtain jail credit information can be challenging and that poor communication with such entities could lead to incorrect release date computations. As mentioned above, these entities include local jails, courthouses, state departments of corrections, Native American reservations, the USMS, and others.

We identified several factors that can make communication with external entities difficult. First, it is not always apparent who has the information the DSCC staff member needs. CC staff members told us that, while phone numbers for most entities are available online, whom to talk to and what communication method they prefer or require is not always apparent. Second, CC staff members told us that the information external entities provide the DSCC may simply be incorrect or contrary to information they previously provided, requiring additional clarification. Third, CC staff members told us that entities vary in their use of terminology. For example, some entities, particularly local jails, use the term "time served" to indicate that the inmate was released after serving all of his or her time. In contrast, the BOP commonly uses this term to indicate all the time the inmate has served up until that point. DSCC officials told us that such terminology differences could lead to a misunderstanding and misapplication of jail credit.

Finally, CC staff members told us that difficulty with establishing contact with some external entities could lead to an incorrect sentence computation and untimely release. Such a scenario is of particular concern for inmates with short sentences. For example, a CC staff member who was computing a sentence for an inmate sentenced to serve 4 months failed to timely follow up with a jail, leading to an untimely release. The staff member was not able to contact the jail on January 9 — the day sentence computation was started — and did not attempt to contact the jail again or complete the sentence computation within the 30-day time frame for short sentences. On March 3 of the same year, the DSCC discovered that the sentence computation had not been completed. Once the DSCC successfully contacted the jail, added the additional jail credit, and completed the computation, the inmate had already over-served 2 days. A senior DSCC official told us that, especially because of the short sentence, the DSCC staff member should have continued to try to contact the jail in the days after January 9.

CC and other DSCC staff members told us that experience computing sentences at the DSCC plays the most important part in being able to successfully communicate with external entities regarding jail credit. Over time, CC staff members develop a rapport with the officials with whom they regularly communicate. They also obtain direct phone numbers, e-mail addresses, preferred communication methods, and other helpful information not always available online. We learned that experienced CC staff members keep this information using their individual rolodexes, electronic documents, or other methods, and share this information with their teammates only on an ad hoc basis.

However, several DSCC staff members told the OIG that it would be useful to have a master document that combines all of the knowledge gained from the team's experience communicating with external entities in the jurisdictions the team covers. We also believe that such a document could be useful if DSCC team members had immediate access to edit its content to keep it up to date. In addition to serving as a more complete list of contacts than each staff member would have separately, it would also assist with retaining knowledge that may otherwise disappear as a result of staff turnover.

Establishing professional relationships is crucial for CC staff members who must obtain accurate and timely information from staffs working at a wide variety of federal, state, and local entities. We found that the CC staff does not receive training focused on establishing and maintaining professional relationships.[23] We believe such training could improve interactions between the DSCC staff and staffs at external entities and could lead to improved access to jail credit information. Training may also improve information sharing between DSCC teammates, with a common goal of ensuring that inmate release dates are calculated correctly. Though the DSCC does not have training focused on establishing and maintaining professional relationships, DSCC managers do counsel and train staff members responsible for errors that led to an untimely release on how the mistakes occurred and how to avoid them in the future. However, we found that the DSCC does not track such counseling or training in an employee's personnel file, which would allow a later reassessment if the same staff member had made a similar error.

Untimely Releases as a Result of Non-DSCC Staff Error

The BOP attributed 30 late untimely releases (out of the 157 in the scope of our review) between 2009 and 2014 to entities other than the DSCC. Our review of the untimely release forms (BP 558 and 623) for these cases indicated that of the entities that were in whole or in part responsible for these untimely releases, BOP institutions were responsible for 14; BOP Residential Reentry Management field offices for 6; Residential Reentry Centers, previously known as Community Corrections Centers, for 3; private contract prisons for 3; and a BOP regional office for 1.[24]

---

[23] Training in interpersonal communication styles could help alleviate computation mistakes. One CC staff member described the importance of building and maintaining a good rapport with representatives from external entities by telling us that a point of contact with whom he had developed an effective working relationship refused to take calls directly from the DSCC staff after having a negative interaction with another DSCC employee. This example shows how poor interpersonal communication among CC staff members can impede timely and accurate sentence computations. A DSCC manager noted that the teams often work with the same jurisdictions regularly; therefore, building rapport can assist teams in obtaining the information necessary to make accurate calculations.

[24] In one of the six untimely releases we attributed to errors of Residential Reentry Management field offices, the error occurred at the local jail to which the field office had assigned the BOP inmate. For 3 of the 30 untimely releases, the BOP attributed error to non-DSCC staffs; but we could not determine whether the USMS, a BOP institution, or both were responsible. BOP documentation indicated that the USMS was at least partially responsible, but the USMS told us that

Continued

The forms for each untimely release, known as Untimely Release Notification (BP 558) and Late Release Notice for United States Probation Service (BP 623), described the reason for the untimely release. Based on our assessment of each narrative, we determined that the four most common descriptions of untimely releases due to non-DSCC staff error were:

1. **Notification or Information Failures.** This includes untimely notifications as well as failures to update, send, or use the correct information. For example, in one situation an inmate incorrectly lost good time credit after a staff member credited it to the wrong inmate. By the time the error was discovered and the good time reapplied, the inmate had over-served 3 days.

2. **Releases the Day After the Correct Release Date, Sometimes without Explanation.** In some of these cases, the BOP was unable to provide us additional information regarding the staff errors that caused the late release or to determine with certainty whether the untimely release was in fact the result of staff error. For example, in one of these cases, after the DSCC updated a sentence computation and notified the facility that the inmate should be released that day, the institution did not release the inmate until the next day and the untimely release report offered no explanation for the delay. According to the BOP, generally when an institution cannot release an inmate on the day he or she is supposed to be released, it can be due to transportation issues, medication requirements, lack of release plans, or incomplete victim and witness notification or *Adam Walsh Child Protection and Safety Act of 2006* review requirements.

3. **Sentence Computation Errors, Primarily by BOP Institutions That Computed Inmate Sentences Prior to the DSCC's Existence, and One Computed by a Contract Facility That Had Yet to Transition Its Sentence Computation Functions to the DSCC.** For example, a private contract facility staff member incorrectly computed an inmate's sentence by misidentifying and misapplying jail credit, resulting in 281 days over-served, the most significant late release due to non-DSCC error.

4. **Failures to Properly Monitor Inmate Release Dates.** In one situation, institution staff failed to run an inmate release roster containing the scheduled release dates of individual inmates, resulting in one inmate over-serving 1 day.

A BOP official told us that the causes of untimely releases are not always identifiable because official documentation sometimes provides inadequate descriptions. We believe that not having thorough and accurate descriptions of the

---

its records did not indicate that the USMS was responsible for the over-served time. This lack of clarity underscores the need for an assessment of untimely releases at the Department level that would allow for a better understanding of how multiple agencies can contribute to untimely releases so that effective solutions for preventing them can be developed.

events leading to untimely release hinders the BOP in identifying and addressing their underlying causes.

The Transition of Sentence Computation Responsibility to the DSCC Appears to Have Reduced the Number of Untimely Releases

The BOP transitioned sentence computations to the DSCC in 2005 in order to consolidate all BOP sentence computation functions, reduce costs, and ensure consistent application of laws and BOP policies. According to the BOP's information, the transfer also appears to have reduced the number of untimely releases due to staff error. As shown in Table 5, between 1999 and 2004 — the 6 years before the DSCC was created in 2005 — there were approximately 344 untimely releases due to staff error (approximately 0.1 percent of the total number of inmates released during the period), compared to 157 during the 6 years between 2009 and 2014 that are the subject of this review (approximately 0.03 percent of the total number of inmates released during this period).[25]

Table 5

Untimely Releases Due to Staff Error before and after Creation of the DSCC
FYs 1999 - 2004 and CYs 2009 - 2014

		Quarter						
	Year	1st	2nd	3rd	4th	Total	Grand Total	% of All Releases
Pre-DSCC	1999	18	9	11	15	53	344	0.10%
	2000	22	17	6		45		
	2001	22	19	22	22	85		
	2002	16	14	12	16	58		
	2003	17	10	16	11	54		
	2004	19	16	14		49		
Post-DSCC	2009	8	11	11	2	32	157	0.03%
	2010	10	5	10	3	28		
	2011	9	3	4	6	22		
	2012	3	6	8	7	24		
	2013	5	4	10	9	28		
	2014	8	3	5	7	23		

Sources: BOP-provided information for FYs 1999 - 2004 and OIG analysis of untimely releases due to staff error as identified by the BOP, CYs 2009 - 2014

[25] The BOP told us that it was unable to provide untimely release information for the fourth quarters of 2000 and 2004 because it had retained some untimely release records for analysis and destroyed others as part of the Records Information Disposal Schedule (they were older than 6 years).

The DSCC staff members we interviewed, including the Chief of the DSCC, told us that because people perform sentence computations, mistakes are inevitable. There is the possibility of human error at every step of the sentence computation process, from initial computation to final release audit. We identified several crucial measures the BOP has in place that help prevent untimely release, including certification and final release audits that double check the initial sentence computation, program reviews of DSCC operations that can result in operational improvements, and processes through which inmates can request a review of their release date. We found that while these measures help to reduce untimely releases due to staff error, they did not eliminate them. As described below, we also identified one additional measure the DSCC could take to help prevent untimely releases due to staff error.

Certification and Final Release Audits

Between 2009 and 2014, 29 of the 157 staff errors that resulted in untimely releases were discovered by certification audits and 19 were discovered by final release audits. We found that final release audits are likely to prevent an untimely release, but only if they occur early enough before an inmate's release date that any reduced sentence time can be accounted for. Currently, the DSCC performs a final release audit 12 months before an inmate's projected release date. Yet for 14 of the 19 errors discovered by final release audits, the untimely release may not have resulted if the final release audit had occurred 18 months before the inmate's release date instead of 12 months.[26] Similarly, 18 of the 19 errors may not have resulted in untimely release if the final release audit had occurred 24 months prior to the release date.[27]

Program Reviews

The BOP's Program Review Division (PRD) and the DSCC routinely conduct program reviews of the DSCC to evaluate trends and identify deficiencies in its operations. Program reviews have resulted in changes to DSCC operations that can help prevent untimely releases. Two PRD reviews, conducted in August of 2009 and September of 2011, rated the DSCC as "acceptable." However, a September 2013 review rated the DSCC as "deficient." The PRD's report stated that the "deficient" rating reflected in part that "initial sentence computations are not always computed and audited within established time frames" and not all source documents "support the sentence computation." To address the former finding, DSCC documentation indicated that the DSCC filled at least four vacant positions

---

[26] We based this determination on the number of over-served days for each inmate. Each of the 14 inmates had less than 6 months of over-served time when the error was discovered during the final release audit, meaning that conducting the final release audits 6 months earlier may have allowed the BOP to avoid the untimely releases.

[27] These four inmates had between 6 and 12 months of over-served time at the time the final release audit discovered the error.

following a period of low staffing levels that the BOP attributed to sequestration and a hiring freeze, and DSCC Section Chiefs began having bi-weekly meetings with managers to ensure the timely completion of certification audits. The DSCC also identified specific teams that had difficulty meeting time frame requirements and placed special emphasis on assisting those teams in complying with the established timeframes. To address the latter finding, according to documentation the BOP provided, the DSCC established a tracking system to identify sentence computation errors and trends, including the tracking of missing source documents; devised a method to assist in naming and saving of source documents; and used bi-weekly meetings to discuss the findings of the tracking system's error report. In September 2014, the PRD closed the 2013 review, stating in a memorandum that the DSCC had resolved all of the deficiencies to the PRD's satisfaction and had put in place administrative controls to prevent recurrence. We did not independently assess the actions the DSCC took that resulted in the PRD closing the review.

Perpetual Audits

"Perpetual audits" are another process the DSCC uses to improve operations and sentence computation accuracy, whereby every month the DSCC staff checks 170 sentence computations (10 for each DSCC team). A DSCC official said that, as a matter of practice, the DSCC uses perpetual audits to identify common mistakes and then conducts training to help DSCC staff avoid making them. In this review, we assessed the monthly perpetual audits that the DSCC conducted between October 2013 and November 2014. Our assessment identified an overall sentence computation error rate of greater than 5 percent for 12 out of 13 months examined. A DSCC official confirmed that the DSCC considers error rates greater than 5 percent to be high. One month's overall error rate was 12 percent. The DSCC told us that to address the high error rates it expanded training for DSCC employees throughout the year by including in the training more complex computation situations and additional information about verifying state information and by conducting training more frequently. The BOP told us that these actions resulted in an error rate of 2.4 percent and an overall rating of "good" on the PRD's January 2015 program review.

Educational Events

We also found that the DSCC conducts educational events related to DSCC operations, such as sentence computation, that may have unmet potential for preventing untimely release. Some of these events bring together officials from the DSCC and non-BOP officials including U.S. District Court Judges, federal Public Defenders, and U.S. Probation Office staff. At these events, the non-DSCC attendees request the topics that are discussed, such as sentence computation, the interaction of federal and non-federal sentences, judicial recommendations, and a general understanding of the role of the DSCC. The DSCC conducted 13 of these educational events between 2009 and 2014.

Historically, the DSCC has not used these events explicitly for the purpose of educating the participants on the means to prevent untimely release, even though they may sometimes offer information that could be helpful in preventing them.

During this review, a DSCC manager expressed the opinion that these education events have the potential to help reduce the number of untimely releases. For example, showing criminal justice officials how conflicting information can lead to an incorrect sentence computation may prompt them to adjust the way they record information. The official also told us that the DSCC has no formal participant feedback process for these events.

We agree that these events could provide a useful forum to discuss topics and share information that could help avoid untimely releases, including topics and information identified by DSCC staff (as opposed to non-DSCC attendees) as pertinent to the effort to prevent untimely releases. The DSCC could further capitalize on these events if it were to identify and invite participation from non-BOP officials whose actions contribute to ensuring timely inmate releases, but who have not previously taken part in these events. We also note that as valuable as these events may already be, the DSCC is missing an opportunity to further enhance their impact and effectiveness by not collecting feedback from participants, which it could use to tailor content to participant needs and interests.

<u>Inquiries by Inmates, Their Families, and Advocates</u>

Inmates, their families, and other advocates have used formal and informal inquiry processes to help bring to light errors made during the sentence computation process. Inmates can, in writing or orally, informally request that the BOP review their release date. Between 2009 and 2014, 54 of the 157 errors that resulted in untimely releases were discovered through inmates' informal requests for review.

Inmates may also at any time file a formal administrative remedy request relating to any aspect of their confinement, including their release date. Administrative remedy requests that challenge a release date have three increasing levels of review: (1) the inmate's institution, (2) the regional office, and (3) the Central Office. Between 2009 and 2014, 6 of the 157 errors that resulted in untimely releases were discovered through the administrative remedy process, 3 were discovered as a result of an attorney's inquiry, and 1 was discovered as a result of a family's inquiry.

Case Studies of Releases Over 1 Year Late

Below we describe the three untimely releases that resulted in inmates spending particularly significant amounts of over-served time in prison. We describe why these late releases occurred, what was done to prevent the mistake from happening again, and the cost to the BOP. In each case, the BOP released the inmate as soon as the error was discovered and the sentence correctly computed.

Case 1: Misapplication of Jail Credit Resulting in 928 Days of Over-served Time

When the DSCC performed the initial sentence computation for this inmate, it did not obtain the relevant state sentencing documents that would have led it to apply jail credit to the inmate's federal sentence. The DSCC did not discover the sentence computation error during the certification audit. Instead, the inmate's inquiry about his release date brought the error to the attention of a BOP regional office. A total of 3 days passed from the date the inmate made the inquiry until the inmate was released. DSCC officials we spoke to said they did not know why the staff did not obtain state sentencing information during the initial sentence computation. The inmate was improperly confined in prison for 928 days, or nearly 3 years, past the correct release date. The result was a serious deprivation of the inmate's liberty and a violation of the court's sentencing order. There also was an additional cost to taxpayers of $66,732 for incarcerating the inmate in a medium security facility for this additional period. The BOP offered no compensation to the inmate, and the inmate did not seek monetary relief. DSCC officials told us that they took no additional action as a result of this error because the staff members responsible for it were no longer employed by the BOP when the error was discovered.

Case 2: Incorrect Primary Jurisdiction Determination Resulting in 541 Days of Over-served Time

When the DSCC performed the initial sentence computation for this inmate, it was unaware of a key document, specifically an amendment to a state judge's previous order that resulted in the release of the inmate from state prison. It was only when the inmate challenged the sentence computation that the DSCC staff discovered the error by finding a reference to the amendment in the online Public Access to Court Electronic Records (PACER) system and, as a result, released the inmate.[28] DSCC officials told us that the CC staff was not aware of the missing document because staff members do not search PACER when they perform sentence computations. DSCC managers told us that the DSCC staff uses PACER only for verifying court orders and reviewing dockets when responding to inquiries and not for sentence computations because doing so would be too cost and labor intensive.[29] As a result of not being aware of the amendment, the DSCC staff incorrectly computed the inmate's sentence based on primary state jurisdiction instead of primary federal jurisdiction. This resulted in jail credit not being applied to the inmate's sentence and the inmate being improperly confined for 541 days, or nearly 1.5 years, past the correct release date, a serious deprivation of the inmate's liberty and a violation of the court's sentencing order. The error also resulted in an additional cost to taxpayers of approximately $40,428 for incarcerating the inmate in a medium security facility for this additional period. The BOP offered no compensation to the inmate, and the inmate did not seek monetary relief. DSCC officials told us that as a result of this untimely release they provided training on the late discovery of information and primary jurisdiction to the team that worked on this inmate's sentence computation.

---

[28] PACER is an electronic public access service that allows users to obtain case and docket information online from federal courts.

[29] The BOP stated that the DSCC staff annually conducts approximately 153,309 initial computations and 91,475 updates to existing computations. Because PACER currently charges 10 cents for every page viewed, viewing one page for each inmate would cost approximately $24,478. This underestimates the total cost because dockets are often longer than one page.

Case 3: Misinterpretation of a Judge's Sentencing Order Resulting in 406 Days of Over-served Time

This inmate was initially convicted on two counts that were to run consecutively. A judge subsequently reduced both counts to a combined 76 months. However, in updating the sentence, the DSCC staff misinterpreted the judge's sentencing order to mean that only the longer of the two counts was to be reduced to 76 months. Both the DSCC staff member performing the computation update and the staff member performing the certification audit to the update made this mistake. As a result, the DSCC scheduled the inmate's release for a significantly later date than it should have. The DSCC discovered the error during the final release audit, approximately 12 months prior to the inmate's incorrect release date. Ultimately, the inmate was improperly confined for 406 days, or over 1 year, past the correct release date. This resulted in a serious deprivation of the inmate's liberty and a violation of the court's sentencing order. It also cost taxpayers approximately $31,619 to incarcerate the inmate in a low security facility for this additional period. The inmate filed a lawsuit against the BOP that ended in a settlement of $175,000. The DSCC Chief's note on the BP 558 form indicated that staff members responsible for the error were reminded to clarify with their supervisor any sentencing order that may be ambiguous.

CONCLUSION AND RECOMMENDATIONS

Conclusion

We found that of the 461,966 inmate releases between 2009 and 2014, the BOP categorized 157 as "untimely" due to staff error and a far greater number — 4,183 — as untimely for other reasons. According to the BOP, the vast majority of untimely releases not due to staff error were due to situations beyond its control, such as amended sentences that resulted in shorter sentences than the time an inmate had already served, compared to the 157 it classified as due to staff error. Data and information we reviewed indicates that other entities may sometimes contribute to untimely releases. Additionally, we found that the BOP does not always have complete information about the circumstances of untimely releases that other entities contributed to. We believe that a review of untimely releases with participation from all relevant entities, both within and outside of the Department, is needed to assess the full range of causes of untimely releases and how best to address those that are in any way preventable.

Our review focused on analyzing the 157 untimely releases that the BOP attributed to staff error. We found that untimely releases due to staff error are rare as a percentage of all inmate releases but, like all untimely releases, can cause very significant harms when they do occur. Late untimely releases inappropriately deprive inmates of their freedom, while early releases result in several potential harms to inmates, their families, and their communities. Both early and late untimely releases contravene court sentencing orders. Moreover, 6 of the 157 releases we examined were untimely by more than a year: we identified early releases of 955, 730, and 368 days and late releases of 928, 541, and 406 days.

While the causes of untimely releases due to staff error are varied, we found that most are the result of an incorrectly computed release date. These computation errors often occur due to the Designation and Sentence Computation Center (DSCC) staff either not getting complete and accurate information from non-BOP entities or not interpreting the information they receive correctly. Although the BOP has several processes in place to prevent untimely releases, we found that there were several steps the BOP could take to further reduce the possibility of untimely release. These include improving, through training and otherwise, the communication tools and skills of the DSCC staff members who must obtain and interpret information from wide variety of federal, state, and local entities outside the DSCC, and implementing additional sentence calculation processing or auditing strategies taking into account that conducting final release audits only 12 months before an inmate's projected release date has led to preventable untimely releases.

Recommendations

To enhance understanding of the circumstances and causes of untimely releases so that the utility of cross-agency solutions for preventing them can be considered, we recommend that the Office of the Deputy Attorney General (ODAG):

1. Work with all relevant entities, both within and outside of the Department, to review the full range of possible reasons for all untimely releases, including those that may not be due to staff error but may still be preventable, and to identify opportunities to reduce the likelihood that they occur.

We make the following recommendations for the BOP to ensure that appropriate notifications are made to the court in cases of untimely release and improve the DSCC's ability to prevent and appropriately handle untimely releases:

2. Work with the ODAG to establish a policy to identify under what circumstances it is appropriate to notify the relevant U.S. Attorney's Office, court official(s), and the affected inmate of an untimely release for any reason, and the reason therefor, and develop a process to ensure that timely notification takes place as appropriate.

3. Ensure that BOP staff members thoroughly and consistently describe and identify the cause of each untimely release in official documentation (such as BP 558 and 623 forms) and use this documentation to support the DSCC's trend analysis for improving training and operations.

4. Implement methods and training to address communication challenges in obtaining accurate and timely jail credit information from judicial as well as other necessary sources.

5. To address the concerns identified in this report that conducting final release audits 12 months before an inmate's projected release date has led to untimely releases due to BOP staff error, explore and implement sentence calculation processing or auditing strategies designed to decrease the likelihood of sentence calculation errors by BOP staff.

6. Incorporate specific untimely release issues and possible solutions into education events, and establish a process for obtaining formal feedback from participants to ensure methods for preventing untimely releases are fully explored.

7. Identify and invite participation from additional non-BOP officials who do not typically participate in education events, but whose actions could help to ensure timely releases, including U.S. District Court Judges, federal Public Defenders, and U.S. Probation Office staff.

METHODOLOGY OF THE OIG REVIEW

The OIG reviewed untimely releases between calendar years (CY) 2009 and 2014. Our review entailed data analysis of BOP untimely release information and interviews with BOP officials knowledgeable about the BOP's process for computing sentences. Of the 4,340 untimely releases that occurred during the scope of our review, we focused primarily on the 157 untimely releases that the BOP identified as having been the result of staff error and determined which entities contributed to the errors. We also reviewed information pertaining to the 4,183 untimely releases not due to staff error, such as the categories of causes for them, but we did not review individual cases.

We obtained untimely release documentation, in the form of Untimely Release Notification (BP 558) and Late Release Notice for United States Probation Service (BP 623) for untimely releases due to staff error from CY 2009 through CY 2014, for Designation and Sentence Computation Center (DSCC) and non-DSCC untimely releases. We compiled this data into a database and analyzed the descriptive statistics. The sample dataset included all untimely release cases the BOP classified as due to staff error during the period of our review; we excluded none from the statistical analysis. Our analysis incorporated a count of the number of cases, the number of total days inmates were released either before or after the correct release date, the average (mean) days under-served or over-served, and its associated standard deviation, among other common descriptive statistical methods. As part of this analysis, we used the narrative portion of the untimely release documentation forms to ascertain information about each untimely release, including the security level of the inmate, how the BOP discovered the error, and the primary factor that caused the error. We also obtained from the BOP the average per-inmate daily cost by security level and year and used it to estimate the costs of the untimely releases due to staff error within our sample. We also reviewed information obtained from e-mail correspondence and phone conversations with non-BOP entities such as the U.S. Marshals Service, the Executive Office for United States Attorneys, and the Administrative Office of the U.S. Courts.

We conducted 28 interviews with BOP staff to learn about the BOP's sentence computation process and perform a qualitative assessment of untimely releases. During these interviews, we inquired about a variety of topics, including explaining or providing context to the data analysis described above. These interviews included non-DSCC staff as well as DSCC staff at various levels within the organization and included Classification and Computation Technicians, Classification and Computation Specialists, management, and the DSCC Chief.

BOP REVIEWS OF THE DESIGNATION AND SENTENCE COMPUTATION CENTER

Beyond audits of individual sentence computations, the BOP, as well as the Designation and Sentence Computation Center (DSCC), conducts program reviews. The BOP's Program Review Division (PRD), tasked with providing oversight of BOP program performance and compliance, reviews the DSCC to evaluate several areas, sentence computations being one of these areas. The PRD conducts program reviews on regular cycles: every 3 years when the DSCC has received an operational rating of "good or superior," 2 years for a rating of "acceptable," and 1 to 1.5 years for a rating of "deficient." When the PRD reviews the DSCC, it issues a report with any specific areas of deficiency and an overall operational rating. The DSCC must respond to the report within 30 days of issuance. Then, within 120 to 150 days of the issuance of the report, the DSCC must conduct its own follow-up review and send a report to the PRD. The follow-up review shows the preliminary results of any actions taken in response to the program review's findings. If no deficiencies are found in the PRD's program review, then no response or follow-up review is required.

During years without program reviews, the DSCC is required to conduct internal reviews of its programs, called operational reviews, in a process similar to that of the PRD's program reviews. Operational reviews are also reported to the PRD and have a similar response and follow-up review process based upon the findings of the operational review.

THE ODAG AND BOP'S RESPONSE TO THE DRAFT REPORT

U. S. Department of Justice

Office of the Deputy Attorney General

Associate Deputy Attorney General   *Washington, D.C. 20530*

May 18, 2016

MEMORANDUM FOR NINA S. PELLETIER
                                ASSISTANT INSPECTOR GENERAL
                                EVALUATION AND INSPECTIONS DIVISION

FROM: Carlos F. Uriarte   *CFU*
                          Associate Deputy Attorney General
                          Office of the Deputy Attorney General

                          Raphael A. Prober   *RAP*
                          Associate Deputy Attorney General
                          Office of the Deputy Attorney General

                          Rae Woods   *CFU for RW*
                          Senior Counsel to the Deputy Attorney General
                          Office of the Deputy Attorney General

                          Thomas R. Kane, Acting Director   *RAP for TRK*
                          Federal Bureau of Prisons

SUBJECT: Response to Draft Report of the Office of the Inspector General: *Review of the
                          Federal Bureau of Prisons' Untimely Release of Inmates*

We appreciate the review undertaken by the Department of Justice (Department) Office of the
Inspector General (OIG) entitled *Review of the Federal Bureau of Prisons' Untimely Release of
Inmates*. The OIG report contains seven recommendations; the Department concurs with all
seven, subject to the comments provided below outlining the Department's continuing concerns
(which are largely definitional in nature). As certain of the recommendations are directed to or
otherwise involve the Office of the Deputy Attorney General (ODAG), and as the balance are
directed to Federal Bureau of Prisons (BOP), this memorandum is being submitted jointly by
ODAG and BOP. With regard to the OIG's formal draft report provided on April 20, 2016,
while neither ODAG nor BOP contest the underlying data or conclusions contained in the report,
the report's presentation and imprecise use of the term "untimely release" continues to be
significantly misleading and blurs the critical distinction between miscalculated prison sentences
due to BOP staff error (157), versus "untimely releases" for other, non-erroneous reasons
(4,183).

By failing to clearly and consistently define terms and distinguish throughout the report between miscalculated sentences due to BOP staff error, and "untimely releases" for non-error reasons, the report fosters a misleading perception that the 4,183 cases reviewed by BOP as "untimely releases" are equivalent in nature with the 157 cases which actually resulted from BOP staff error, which is absolutely not the case. In fact, many of those 4,183 cases reviewed by BOP as "untimely releases" are entirely appropriate releases, as described in further detail below. Stated affirmatively, OIG's review revealed BOP's accuracy rate for sentence calculations during the timeframe reviewed to be 99.97%.

Recommendation 1: *To the Office of the Deputy Attorney General, to work with all relevant entities, both within and outside of the Department, to review the full range of possible reasons for all untimely releases, including those that may not be due to staff error but may still be preventable, and to identify opportunities to reduce the likelihood that they occur.*

Response: ODAG concurs with Recommendation 1, and agrees to look at the full range of untimely releases, but will focus its efforts on trying to understand those untimely releases that are both preventable and improper. As discussed in the report, the vast majority (4,183) of "untimely releases" are the result of court initiated actions (i.e., original, amended, and/or vacated court orders), and are not errors of any type. It is, therefore, presumed that the courts' orders, and their consequences, were intentional. Insofar as calculation, and recalculation, of inmates' sentences consistent with valid court orders is in the ordinary course of business, there is no demonstrated need for ODAG to work to "reduce the likelihood" of preventing such occurrences.

Recommendation 2: *To BOP, to work with ODAG to establish a policy to identify under what circumstances it is appropriate to notify the relevant U.S. Attorney's Office and/or court official(s), and the affected inmate of an untimely release for any reason, and the reason therefore, of an untimely release for any reason including but not limited to those caused by staff error.*

Response: BOP agrees with this recommendation, and will work with ODAG to establish, or revise, its policy to identify under what circumstances it is appropriate to notify the relevant U.S. Attorney's offices and/or court officials(s), and the affected inmate, and develop a process to ensure that timely notification occurs.

Recommendation 3: *To BOP, to ensure that BOP staff members thoroughly and consistently describe and identify the cause of each untimely release in official documentation (such as BP 558 and 623 forms) and use this documentation to support the DSCC's trend analysis for improving training and operations.*

Response: BOP agrees with this recommendation and will explore methods for consistently describing and identifying the cause of untimely releases due to staff error in official documentation, for use in support of DSCC trend analysis for improving training and operations.

Recommendation 4: *To BOP, to implement methods and training to address communication challenges in obtaining accurate and timely jail credit information from judicial as well as other* *necessary sources.*

Response: BOP agrees with this recommendation and will explore enhanced methods and training to obtain accurate and timely jail credit information from judicial, as well as other necessary sources.

Recommendation 5: *To BOP, to address the concerns identified in this report that conducting final release audits 12 months before an inmate's projected release date has led to untimely releases due to BOP staff error, explore and implement sentence calculation processing or auditing strategies designed to decrease the likelihood of sentence calculation errors by BOP staff.*

Response: BOP agrees with this recommendation, and will explore and implement sentence calculation processing or auditing strategies designed to decrease the likelihood of sentence calculation errors by BOP staff.

Recommendation 6: *To BOP, incorporate specific untimely release issues and possible solutions into education events, and establish a process for obtaining formal feedback from participants to ensure methods for preventing untimely release are fully explored.*

Response: BOP agrees with this recommendation and will incorporate untimely release issues related to staff error into education events and request feedback from participants to ensure methods of preventing such.

Recommendation 7: *To BOP, identify and invite participation from additional non-BOP officials who do not typically participate in education events, but whose actions could help to ensure timely releases, including U.S. District Court Judges, federal Public Defenders, and U.S. Probation Office staff.*

Response: BOP agrees with this recommendation and will explore identifying and inviting non-BOP representatives from the referenced offices to participate in BOP educational events. Additionally, BOP's response to this recommendation will include BOP/DSCC staff participation in educational events coordinated by those non-BOP offices.

OIG ANALYSIS OF THE ODAG AND BOP's RESPONSE

The OIG provided a draft of this report to the Office of the Deputy Attorney General (ODAG) and the BOP for their comments. The ODAG and BOP's response is included in Appendix 3 of this report. Below, we discuss the OIG's analysis of the ODAG and BOP's response and the actions necessary to close the recommendations.

Recommendation 1: Work with all relevant entities, both within and outside of the Department, to review the full range of possible reasons for all untimely releases, including those that may not be due to staff error but may still be preventable, and to identify opportunities to reduce the likelihood that they occur.

Status: Resolved.

ODAG and BOP Response: The ODAG concurred with the recommendation and stated that it agrees to look at the full range of untimely releases while focusing on trying to understand those untimely releases that are both preventable and improper. The ODAG referred to information in the report showing that the vast majority of releases that the BOP classifies as "untimely" are the result of court initiated actions rather than error, noting that there is no demonstrated need for the ODAG to reduce the likelihood of preventing non-erroneous occurrences.

OIG Analysis: The ODAG's planned actions are responsive to the recommendation, as long as its review includes a complete assessment of what constitutes a "preventable and improper" untimely release.

In their comments, the ODAG and BOP referred to continuing definitional concerns with our report pertaining to distinguishing between untimely releases due to miscalculated prison sentences resulting from BOP staff error on the one hand, and those due to other non-erroneous reasons on the other hand. In this report, we use the term "untimely release" the way the BOP currently uses it, as a broad description of all instances in which an inmate was not released on his or her correct date, including when this occurs for non-erroneous reasons. The term therefore includes instances we refer to as technicalities, such as when the "correct date" is established retroactively because of a court's sentencing adjustments.

Because the BOP's definition of "untimely release" blurs the distinction between proper and improper, and between preventable and unpreventable, we believe that examining, and possibly revising, the definition of untimely release could be a useful aspect of the ODAG's assessment. But, at a minimum, the ODAG's assessment should avoid artificially narrowing the universe of untimely releases at issue, since the intent of our recommendation is for the ODAG, BOP, and all other stakeholders to explore, collaboratively, all the ways untimely releases occur so that they can identify and implement methods to prevent them and avoid as many untimely releases as possible.

Additionally, we noted in our report that it was beyond the scope of our review to assess the circumstances of untimely releases not due to staff error, of which the BOP's records indicate there were more than 4,000. To the extent that the ODAG and BOP's joint response is intended to imply that any particular portion, or all, of those more than 4,000 untimely releases were not the result of an error, or not preventable, we emphasize our finding that "the BOP does not always have complete information about the circumstances of untimely releases to which other entities contribute." Therefore, we do not believe that the ODAG should define the scope of the multiagency review at the outset in a manner that would categorically exclude cases about which the BOP lacks complete information. While we agree that there is no need — and no way — to prevent releases that are "untimely" *only* because of a retroactive sentence adjustment, we believe a full review is needed because of the wide range of factors that may contribute to untimely releases, some of which may currently be unknown to the ODAG, the BOP, or other stakeholders, and may be preventable.

By August 31, 2016, please provide the ODAG's plan for looking into the full range of untimely releases, including its framework for defining and identifying which untimely releases are preventable and improper, as well as a list of the agencies it plans to include in its review.

Recommendation 2: Work with the ODAG to establish a policy to identify under what circumstances it is appropriate to notify the relevant U.S. Attorney's Office, court official(s), and the affected inmate of an untimely release for any reason, and the reason therefor, and develop a process to ensure that timely notification takes place as appropriate.

Status: Resolved.

ODAG and BOP Response: The BOP stated that it agrees with this recommendation and that it will work with the ODAG to establish, or revise, its policy to identify the circumstances under which it is appropriate to notify the relevant U.S. Attorney's Office and/or court officials(s), and the affected inmate, and will develop a process to ensure that timely notification occurs.

OIG Analysis: The BOP's planned actions are responsive to the recommendation. By August 31, 2016, please provide the policy and/or policy changes that identify the circumstances of untimely release under which it is appropriate to notify the relevant U.S. Attorney's Office, court officials(s), and the affected inmate, including the reason for the untimely release, as well as documentation of the process that will ensure that timely notification occurs.

Recommendation 3: Ensure that BOP staff members thoroughly and consistently describe and identify the cause of each untimely release in official documentation (such as BP 558 and 623 forms) and use this documentation to support the Designation and Sentence Computation Center's (DSCC) trend analysis for improving training and operations.

Status: Resolved.

ODAG and BOP Response: The BOP stated that it agrees with this recommendation and will explore methods for consistently describing and identifying the cause of untimely releases due to staff error in official documentation.

OIG Analysis: The BOP's response is partially responsive to the recommendation. To be fully responsive to this recommendation, the BOP must also explore methods for consistently describing and identifying in official documentation the causes of untimely releases *not* due to staff error. We note that it will not always be possible to completely document untimely releases beyond the BOP's control. However, it is still important to enhance such documentation where possible because this information can also be useful in trend analysis for improving training and operations. By August 31, 2016, please provide documentation of the methods developed for consistently describing and identifying the cause of all untimely releases.

Recommendation 4: Implement methods and training to address communication challenges in obtaining accurate and timely jail credit information from judicial as well as other necessary sources.

Status: Resolved.

ODAG and BOP Response: The BOP stated that it agrees with this recommendation and will explore enhanced methods and training to obtain accurate and timely jail credit information from judicial as well as other necessary sources.

OIG Analysis: The BOP's planned actions are responsive to the recommendation. By August 31, 2016, please provide documentation of the enhanced methods and training explored — indicating which of them the BOP plans to implement — to obtain accurate and timely jail credit information from judicial as well as other necessary sources.

Recommendation 5: To address the concerns identified in this report that conducting final release audits 12 months before an inmate's projected release date has led to untimely releases due to BOP staff error, explore and implement sentence calculation processing or auditing strategies designed to decrease the likelihood of sentence calculation errors by BOP staff.

Status: Resolved.

ODAG and BOP Response: The BOP stated that it agrees with the recommendation and that it will explore and implement sentence calculation processing or auditing strategies designed to decrease the likelihood of sentence calculation errors by BOP staff.

OIG Analysis: The BOP's planned actions are responsive to the recommendation. By August 31, 2016, please provide documentation of sentence calculation processing or auditing strategies that have been implemented and are designed to decrease the likelihood of sentence calculation errors by BOP staff.

Recommendation 6: Incorporate specific untimely release issues and possible solutions into education events, and establish a process for obtaining formal feedback from participants to ensure methods for preventing untimely releases are fully explored.

Status: Resolved.

ODAG and BOP Response: The BOP stated that it agrees with the recommendation and that it will incorporate untimely release issues related to staff error into education events and will request feedback from participants to ensure methods of preventing such.

OIG Analysis: The BOP's response is partially responsive to the recommendation. To be fully responsive to this recommendation, the BOP must also incorporate into education events any untimely release issues identified in the ODAG's multiagency review or by the BOP that are related to non-staff errors. In fact, because the purpose of these events is to educate representatives from criminal justice agencies outside of the BOP, these events are specifically an opportunity to inform representatives from other agencies about what they can do that would reduce the likelihood of untimely releases. By August 31, 2016, please provide a list of education events conducted or planned since the issuance of this report, a list of the untimely release issues incorporated into each event, and documentation of the process for requesting feedback.

Recommendation 7: Identify and invite participation from additional non-BOP officials who do not typically participate in education events, but whose actions could help to ensure timely releases, including U.S. District Court Judges, federal Public Defenders, and U.S. Probation Office staff.

Status: Resolved.

ODAG and BOP Response: The BOP stated that it agrees with this recommendation and that it will explore identifying and inviting non-BOP representatives from referenced offices to participate in BOP educational events and that it will include BOP/DSCC staff in educational events coordinated by those non-BOP offices.

OIG Analysis: The BOP's response is responsive to the recommendation. By August 31, 2016, please provide documentation of which non-BOP representatives the BOP has invited or has identified to invite to BOP educational events, a list of planned events through 2017, and an indication of which events coordinated by non-BOP offices the BOP has identified for BOP/DSCC staff to participate in.